MW00737202

Ideas in Reality

Making Your Ideas Happen

Stefania Lucchetti

Restless Travellers Publishing

Restless Travellers Publishing Limited
(www.restlesstravellerspublishing.com)
38th Floor, Tower One, Lippo Centre,
89 Queensway, Hong Kong, Hong Kong SAR

ISBN: 978-988-99758-6-9

© 2011 Stefania Lucchetti

Printed in Canada, March 2011

Also by Stefania Lucchetti:

The Principle of Relevance, RT Publishing, Hong Kong, 2010

Meditation for Busy Minds, RT Publishing, Hong Kong 2011

The Own Your Time Series (www.ownyourtimeseries.com)

To my son Sky, may he always be able to make his dreams come true

Contents

Acknowledgments 7

Introduction 9

Chapter 1 Creativity at Work 13

Chapter 2 A lesson from chemistry 20

Chapter 3 The Ideation 25

Chapter 4 The Conceptualization 41

Chapter 5 The Materialization 53

Chapter 6 Putting Everything Into Motion 81

Acknowledgments

Thank you to all the readers who offered feedback on the evolving manuscript. Thank you to the readers of my first book, *The Principle of Relevance,* for encouraging me to write more. Thank you to my clients and friends who have made the ideas in this book come alive. Thank you to the magic Steve Harrison and his team for putting together a stellar program that allows for no more excuses. Thank you to Deborah Englander for precision editing. Thank you to Brian Feinblum for bringing on the limelight.

A very special thank you to Mary Testin for sharing her long term experience as a chemistry teacher to help me describe the consolidation process.

Thank you to Ram Biala for suggesting the powerful title: Ideas in Reality.

And most of all, thank you to my husband, my partner in crime and in business, who is the first person I turn to when I want to make my ideas become reality.

Introduction

Among the questions that I am asked most frequently are: "How do you do it all? How do you so easily put in place your ideas? How do you get ideas in the first place and actually manage to make them happen?"

In today's extremely specialized world, it is very common to categorize people as being either gifted creators or great executors, but rarely both. While it is true that most people have a predominant attitude or preference for either the creative aspect or the execution aspect, there is absolutely no reason that prevents someone from being great at both.

However, becoming skillful at both, in this age of increasing specialization, requires going against popular culture.

Creatively oriented people (whether artists or entrepreneurs), while usually admired in the mature part of their life, often go through very difficult time while growing up. This can be explained by the standardized school system which rarely develops curiosity, delight in exploration and ambiguity and asking questions. The system is based on teaching the student to put everything into structure, logic and well known formats Left brain thinking, that is, analytical – logical thinking, is always preferred.

For this same reason, people who are balanced or already logically oriented, rarely find in school (or work) any incentive to develop the skill of "idea creation". Even in activities which should fall under the artistic batch, such as playing an instrument, children are taught to follow rules and play the tune, but rarely to improvise.

Fortunately, this means that if you think you are not creative, it maybe that you just have not have had an opportunity to explore this side of yourself, and this book is for you.

On the other hand, you may be one of those fortunate people who have a knack for idea generation, but poor follow up skills. How many times have you thought of a really fantastic idea? Maybe it was something that would revolutionize the way your office operates. Or perhaps it was a great product that would appeal to millions of people worldwide. Perhaps, you have been planning to start your own business for a while, or write a book, or simply be able to regularly implement fresh ideas in your life, like learning a new sport, creating a garden or organizing your time in a certain way. This book is also for you.

There is a way to be consistently great at both generating and executing ideas. As you read through this book, you will learn strategies to accomplish both these goals.

I would like you to read this book once, in its entirety, and then go back to read it one more time, applying what you have learned. I would also like to hear from you – how your ideas are becoming reality, how this book has helped you achieve your dreams (there is a contact form on my website www.stefanialucchetti.com, I encourage you to use it and I will try to respond to all messages personally).

Chapter 1

Creativity at Work

Might "genius" be a potential we all share, each of us with our own unique capacity for creativity, requiring only the power of sustained attention to unlock it?

B. Allan Wallace, PH.D., The Attention Revolution, 2006

You may be naturally creative or you may have developed your creativity through lateral thinking exercises, study, brainstorming sessions and creativity coaching. Creativity expresses itself in many different ways: in the production of works of art, writing, in the generation of business ideas or ideas that solve professional or personal issues, major or small, and generally make your life easier and more enjoyable.

Often, however, you may find that the process of transforming an idea into reality eludes you and you are left off wondering whether this is due to a lack of execution skills. Given that most people are good at execution in their jobs, often a lack of idea implementation is interpreted as a lack of creativity. You may think you are not creative enough to produce ideas that are worth executing. This is, more often than not, just an excuse we tell ourselves to avoid really understanding the process of generating ideas and putting them to practice.

A creative journey often begins with a spark in your mind. Then the challenge is to make it happen, to transform it into reality, to mould it into something alive and "touchable" or "usable" in the outside world.

Then, the process of turning that idea into reality is completely different and requires the mind to work at a very different level. It is difficult for a creative mind to accept that an inspiring, creative sprout then needs to be developed much like the completion of an administrative task. However, trying to transform the creative idea into reality requires a completely different mode and mindset than that which has produced the idea. Making ideas happen requires organization and relentless execution.

At the opposite end of the spectrum, if you have an execution oriented, logical mind, you might find it difficult to access your ideas, and may have concluded that you are just not creative. This happens for the same reason: ideas and the execution of ideas require a completely different mindset. The reality is that you certainly have ideas but you let them sit in the back of your mind without acknowledging and doing something with them.

Why does this happen?

The creative world seems to be at odds with the organized world. There is creativity on one side and productivity on the other. Generating ideas is often at odds with their execution. The common misconception is that some people are great at being creative, and some people are great at being organized and productive, but no one can be both.

The capacity to generate ideas and make them happen is a gift that we all have. You are gifted with virtually unlimited potential for learning and creativity. The ability to access this creativity, however, which is at its maximum potential in small children, is often lost as we grow up.

A study carried out on the artistic expression of small children compared to middle school children and published by the journal Studies in Art Education in 1997 by a researcher of Harvard Project Zero has shown how there is a loss of creativity in children as they progress with their schooling, which is only developed again in those adults who choose to pursue an artistic career.

Therefore, if you believe you are not creative, it simply means you have become lazy and forgotten how to tap into your brain's creative potential.

The same principle applies for intelligence. In a statistical review of more than 200 studies of IQ published in the journal Nature, Bernard Devlin concluded that genes account for no more than 48% of IQ. The rest is a function of environment and education.

Another myth is that each one of us possesses only, or primarily one type of intelligence. In fact, the human brain is like a multidimensional instrument that can play an infinite number of musical pieces, sometimes one at the time and sometimes simultaneously.

In *Frames of Mind, The Theory of Multiple Intelligences* Howard Garner categorized intelligence into seven different types:

1. logical mathematical
2. verbal-linguistic
3. spatial- mechanical
4. musical
5. bodily- kinaesthetic
6. interpersonal – social

7. intrapersonal (self knowledge)

Each of these aspects of intelligence can be developed throughout life so that it becomes as strong as the others. Everyone can develop and use all these forms of intelligence, although different situations will require the use of one aspect more than another.

With the new knowledge about the human brain now available, it should be widely accepted that anyone can both generate ideas and make them happen. Doing so, however, requires using a method and you are the only one who can be learn and master this method.

A word of caution is necessary here. Most individuals rarely find support in their environment (social family or corporate) when they have a new idea.

It is a situation that I have seen over and over again and that can be explained by two reasons. First, society, and business for the most part, thrives on conformity and routine. This does not encourage creativity which is by definition an assumptions-breaking process. Creative ideas are often generated when one discards preconceived assumptions and attempts a new approach or method that often seems unthinkable to others.

However, satisfying an existing customer through a well known method is usually far easier, more efficient and less energy consuming than pursuing a new idea, which is often time consuming, uneconomical, and risky.

Second, everyone has seen the concept of a new idea often whither in the actual pursuit of it, without any apparent reason, and therefore there is a general wariness towards believing that a new idea can become reality.

A few years ago while working in a corporate environment, one of my colleagues (a lawyer) came up with a new, interesting business idea. He discussed it with the team because he wanted some constructive feedback (and perhaps some encouragement) before proposing it to the relevant business stakeholders. The reactions he received were of this sort: "If no one else has come up with it yet, why should you? You are not even a business person, you are a lawyer!" Others said, "Don't you think that if it were such a great idea someone else would have already had it?" or "How are you going to have time to deal with this?"

In the end, he did not feel confident enough to submit his idea, and my encouragement was not enough to persuade him. I felt sad and angry for him, but also realized that he had encountered the normal, ordinary reactions that all new ideas face.

It is truly a gift for individuals to be able to hold a vision against other people's limited perspective.

The truth is that society is keen on maintaining the *status quo* and this is reflected in your behaviour. This tendency, which has a lot to do with self preservation, has been described as "the lizard brain" by the well known author, marketing guru and change agent Seth Godin.

Whenever you are on the verge of taking an important step that will change your life in some minor or major way (getting married, shipping out a manuscript to a publisher, giving a presentation) you get cold feet and you may end up sabotaging yourself.

Only if you choose to commit to action without regard for success or failure, or whether you have external support or not, can you avoid this set of excuses.

Chapter 2

A Lesson From Chemistry

The metaphor is perhaps one of man's most fruitful potentialities. Its efficacy verges on magic, and it seems a tool for creation which God forgot inside one of His creatures when He made him.

José Ortega y Gasset, in The Dehumanization of Art (1925)

Why do those ideas never happen?

Think back to your high school chemistry classes. Do you remember the process of condensation and the states of matter. You certainly recall that matter can vary in state from gas, liquid and solid.

States of matter change as energy and motion of particles change. When energy decreases, an attraction among particles develops, and matter condenses from gas, to liquid, into solid.

Take water for example. At low temperatures, we find it as ice. The molecules are in a low energy state, locked in a crystal structure with special bonds (hydrogen bonds) between molecules, low energy, but low randomness too. As the temperature increases, the crystal melts into water and molecules can run around. As the temperature continues to increase, water boils and becomes a gas. The particles are free to go where they will: freedom! But also chaos!

Conversely, if the temperature decreases, the particles succumb to a lower energy state and condense. If the temperature becomes still colder, almost all freedom is lost as the water molecules settle into a predetermined, orderly crystal. Energy is low and the molecules are only allowed to wiggle a little within their places.

Where am I going with this? The process of turning an idea into reality is similar to the conversion process of matter from gas into liquid and then into solid. You will probably balk at this notion but read closely and I think you'll be persuaded.

Take a look at the characteristics of the three stages of matter. We have:

Gas: which is high energy, fast moving, maximum chaos, uncontainable;

Liquid: which is medium energy, flexible, containable; and

Solid: which is low energy, rigid, mostly fixed in form.

Now, the process of turning an idea into reality requires three steps:

1. *First step*: **generating** the idea

2. *Second step*: **conceptualizing** the idea into thought

3. *Third step*: **materializing** that idea in the physical plane.

How is this similar to the process of condensation?

1. **First step: idea generation**. An idea is like matter at the gaseous phase. It is fast moving, immediate, abstract and uncontainable.

2. **Second step: conceptualizing the idea into thought**. Thought is like matter at the liquid state. It is touchable, contained, flexible and fluid.

3. **Third step: materializing that idea in the physical plane**. The materialization of an idea - then thought - into the physical plane is like bringing matter to the solid state. It is rigid and it has structure and form.

How is this relevant to our discussion? Bringing an idea down to thought and then to reality requires the mind to work at very different energy, or frequency levels. This means that you cannot approach the idea generation phase in the same state of mind by applying the same techniques and skills you use for the materialization phase because you are dealing with a completely different "state" of your idea.

Imagine your ideas in their generation phase as matter at the gaseous state. They move at a very high frequency level and they are tough to catch. The most difficult thing to do at this stage is to "catch" those ideas, thereby becoming fully aware of them.

Ideas then need to be condensed into a lower frequency level, the liquid state - or thought. At this stage, ideas need to be conceptualized. This is when you need to record the ideas and transform them into comprehensible thoughts.

Finally, ideas need to be further condensed into matter, compressing them down to a lower energetic level, where they become fixed, containable, and have a form.

The chemical process of transforming your ideas into reality therefore requires you to shift between very different levels! It is probably difficult to accept that, in fact, a creative sprout which feels so much like divine inspiration then needs to be condensed and compressed, at a level where you work on it at the same level as an administrative task. Trying to produce the creative idea in the same mode as it was formed is the near fatal mistake that most people make when going from idea generation to execution.

Phase	You can imagine it as	Characteristics
Idea generation	Gas	Fast moving Immediate Abstract Uncontainable
Idea conceptualization	Liquid	Touchable Containable Flexible Fluid
Idea materialization	Solid	Rigid Structure Form

Let's see how the process works in detail.

Chapter 3

The Ideation

These ideas did not come in any verbal formulation. I rarely think in words at all. An idea comes, and I may try to express it in words afterward.

Albert Einstein, Quoted in H Eves Mathematical Circles Adieu (Boston 1977).

Based on its etymology, the word "creativity" simply means the act of making something new.

Although a simple concept, the creative process is constantly the object of studies from the perspective of psychology, psychometrics, cognitive science, philosophy, aesthetics, history, economics, design research, business and management. There is not however a single, scientific, commonly accepted definition of creativity, a consent on its origins, nor a standardized measurement technique.

Creativity has been attributed variously to divine intervention, cognitive processes, the social environment, personality traits, even accident. Some say it is a trait we are born with; others say it can be taught and learned.

Insight: What are the distinctive characters of a highly creative mind?

In How to Think Like Leonardo Da Vinci, author Michael J. Gelbl summarizes the principles that inspired the life of all round artist, scientist and humanist Leonardo da Vinci:

Curiosity – an insatiably curious approach to life and an unrelenting quest for continuous learning. This is the desire to know, learn and grow.

Demonstration – a commitment to test knowledge through experience, persistence and a willingness to learn from mistakes. This means thinking for yourself and freeing your mind.

Sensory power – continual refinement of the senses and sensory awareness, especially sight, as a means to enliven and enrich experience

Sfumato – a willingness to embrace ambiguity, paradox, and uncertainty. "Confusion endurance" is the most distinctive trait of highly creative people.

Art/Science – the development of balance between science and art, logic and imagination. Whole brain thinking

Physical agility – the cultivation of trace, fitness and poise

Connection – a recognition of and appreciation for the interconnectedness of all things and phenomena. Systems thinking. An appreciation for patterns, relationships, connections and systems. Understanding how your dreams goals values and highest aspirations can be integrated into your daily life.

Studies of the lives of inventors, artists and other creative people reveal a common trait that is widely recognized. The creative genius occurs during a moment of reflection, of inward turning, or of quiet. It happens during sleep, while taking a walk, or enjoying an absentminded shower, for example. It often happens during a moment of stillness following a great spurt of activity, as if it were a result of the polarized interaction between action and stillness.

Think about a situation when you were struggling with a problem and could not solve it. Then suddenly, while you are showering, walking outside, resting in bed, driving or listening to music, a seemingly perfect solution to your problem leaps into your mind - and proves to be exactly right. Few people claim they get their best ideas at work. What happens in these cases?

Possibly, it could be argued that all creativity and inventiveness occurs when a person is able to, consciously or unconsciously, leave the boundaries of the logical mind, relax and enter a different level of consciousness. This different level of consciousness, which psychologists call subconscious and yogis call higher consciousness, is that restful yet focused state you are in when you are completely relaxed while at the same time completely focused in what you are doing. Think for example of times when you have enjoyed a blissful hot shower or a slow swim in spectacular waters. This state of consciousness is so difficult to describe and understand because it is beyond thought. The frequency and the speed of the concepts that go through your mind at this stage are too fast for thought.

Albert Einstein used to say that he never thought in words. Words are a means of translating ideas into concepts that can be shared with other people, but they are too slow for ideas, which come in direct perceptions, flashes of wisdom, images and feelings, which are then later translated into words by the mind as a form of communication.

Everyone is capable of producing ideas. The problem is not a lack of capacity for idea generation. Instead, it is that ideas are produced in a state of consciousness that is beyond thought so you may often not be aware of those ideas because you are immersed in thoughts, which – as we have seen – are lower and slower. Ideas might float through your mind so fast that you do not recognize them, or take notice of them, or if you do, you soon forget them. Even if you are able to take notice of an idea, you might forget it immediately, just as you probably struggle to remember your dreams.

Insight: Higher Consciousness

What do we mean by "a different state of consciousness" or "higher consciousness?" It is a realm of awareness beyond logical thinking consciousness. Higher consciousness is the awareness at the source of your thinking, feeling, and acting.

This higher consciousness is the source of your normal awareness, your ability to think, feel, act, and to be sensitive to your outer world.

Ideas are produced in the realm of higher consciousness and they are quicker than thought. However this state can only be entered when your body is calm and your thoughts and feelings turn inwards.

Generating ideas

The common conception is that you need to feel the creative muse in order to be creative. But the reality is that inspiration is always within you and it is up to you to find it instead of waiting for it to find you.

We have just explained that the most comment trait to creativity is that it manifests in open, relaxed situations: in the shower, while amidst nature, sleeping, exercising, waiting for someone, driving, or in transition between places, such as when riding an elevator. There is very little likelihood that you will get creative ideas while sitting in front of your desk in a cubicle. After all, how do you expect to think creatively and innovatively if you spend your time clicking back and forth between emails and browser windows?

The idea generation process usually starts when you are trying to solve a problem, or when you become inspired by something new you perceive in your environment. Therefore, in order to expand your capacity for generating ideas you need to have two things:

1.   Various and deep interests.   You will not generate ideas if you don't face new problems or if you do the same repetitive

tasks day after day. And you will not generate ideas if you do not expose yourself to new stimulus such as new environments, new activities, new music, and new people.

2.   Mental space to allow ideas to be generated. Remember, ideas are like gaseous matter which needs space to expand. If you don't have mental space, you will not be able to generate ideas.

In my corporate seminars on leadership and time management, I often speak of the importance of maintaining "mental bandwidth" as a source of the ability to create ideas, explore opportunities and see the big picture. In order to do this, you have to become very disciplined about where you choose to focus your attention. You must make conscious choices about your daily information diet, avoiding information overload and being at all times a master of your own time. By learning how to relax and intentionally quiet the mind, you can actually train creativity, just like a muscle.

Becoming aware of your best idea generation times and places and creating some ritual around them is also very important. When you are conscious of the best conditions for your creativity, you can prepare yourself for creativity by creating anchors, or small rituals, that take you into that same mental zone.   A particular scent or, a posture, something you say to yourself, something you like to read, something that reminds you of a particular environment can help you get into a creative zone effortlessly. For example, when I want to write, I clear my desk and diffuse my favourite aromatherapy scent (lavender and ylang ylang).

Becoming Aware of Ideas

Ideas arrive as direct perceptions, flashes, glimpses of images, feelings, insights or all of these at the same time.

They are so fast – faster than thought – that in order to become aware of them, you need to be able to access and recognize a different state of consciousness from streaming thought. You need to be able to watch and observe your thoughts and emotions as a witness and not be carried away by them. The technique that trains you to do this is meditation.

When, through a regular practice of meditation, you become aware of your own thoughts, you will become aware of your creative processes as well, and you will be surprised at how many more of these thoughts you can recall and put to use. I suggest you write down your thoughts in a journal. When unaware, you often don't know what your thoughts are.

Everyone generates idea all the time, but usually, you're not attune and aware of these mental processes which makes it difficult to recognize and catch those ideas as they appear.

Insight: Meditation

In daily life, you are engaged by objects of experiences -- your physical surroundings, the people you engage with, intellectual stimulation and inputs you need to process, your thoughts in relation to those inputs. In the modern world, these objects of experience are not only ever-present, but also tend to change and shift at very high speed.

This causes the mind to be totally engrossed in these objects of experience, sometimes losing itself in them.

In meditation, the reference point is shifted from the object of experience inwardly to the witness of that same experience.

In the meditation process, you become aware of your body, then your mind, then your emotions and then, ultimately, to the awareness, the witness consciousness, behind all these three aspects of your being.

Meditation allows you to intentionally enter an altered state of consciousness that is more focused and more profound than ordinary consciousness and develops unparalleled self awareness. Because you learn to watch those experiences, you become aware of them and their effects so that eventually you are able to control them.

If you are interested in learning more about meditation, and how it can empower you, I invite you to read my book "Meditation for Busy Minds - And How It Can Make You a Better Leader".

THE ROADMAP TO
BOOST YOUR IDEA-GENERATION POTENTIAL

Becoming Aware of Your Idea Generation Potential

Few people claim to get their best ideas at work. You must become aware of where you are when you get your best ideas. Is it while you are resting in bed, walking outside, listening to music while driving or while, relaxing in the shower or bath? Are you alone or with others? Are you outdoors or indoors?

Usually empty, open large spaces with natural stimuli are best for inducing a creative state of mind. Take frequent walks or runs outside or sit on an open terrace. The key is to be outside

When you find yourself at your most creative, say something to yourself, assume a specific body posture or take a small object in your hands (the object must be portable: you must be able to carry it around with you at all times). Do the same thing when you want to easily shift in a creative zone at any other time. This process is called "anchoring." The anchor (the words you say, the posture you take, the object you touch) helps your body and brain remember the creative zone.

Questions For You

When and where do you get your best ideas?

_____

_____

_____

_____

_____

What are you going to use as anchor? What will you say to yourself? What posture will you take? What portable object or scent will you use?

_____

_____

_____

_____

_____

Making Space

Creativity thrives in bright, unstructured, open spaces. Every day, spend some time outdoors. Walk, exercise or meditate in nature, or just slowly sip a cup of coffee while sitting on a terrace.

Take a one hour break from emails before going to bed and don/t read emails first thing in the morning. Have a shower, eat breakfast, have a chat with someone in your family, then - and only then - rush to your loved blackberry or iphone. You will find that the world will still be there. Your emails will be there as well. But you will have created a significant mental space in your day.

While working or studying, take a break every hour. Go for a walk, look out of the window, close your eyes, listen to some music or doodle.

Do at least one activity during the day in which you allow your attention to be fully absorbed for at least an hour without checking the time. This period should not include watching TV.

Pause before starting an activity. When the telephone rings, stop and take a breath before answering. While the computer boots, close your eyes for a few seconds and take a breath. Before stepping into your car or subway, stop, take a breath and look around. It will feel like time is rebooting.

Create small rituals for yourself that involve a time for quiet contemplation. These can include walking, listening to music, reading a novel, enjoying a cup of coffee in the sunshine or not doing anything at all.

Digital information overload is the first cause of shrinking of mental bandwidth. Become your information dietician, examine your daily information intake and consider whether your info diet needs fine tuning. In particular, make a conscious decision and commitment to turn off your blackberry, iphone, computers and television at certain specific hours of the day.

Questions For You

What are those hours of the day or situations where you can take a break from technology?

_____

_____

_____

_____

_____

What will you do in your buffer times (while waiting for someone to join you for lunch, while waiting for transportation, in a taxi etc) instead of looking at your blackberry? (Ideas: carry a book with you and read, think, doodle, write ideas in you notebook)

_____

_____

_____

_____

_____

Expanding Your Outlook

When you read or hear about something new, make a note of it and then look it up.

Read.

Seek out different perspectives

Make a list of three new things you want to try in the next 12 months. Try out one at the time.

Make sure to take time, at least twice a week for activities that are slow, engaging, inspiring, thought provoking and which spur creativities.

Questions For You

Which new activities or experiences will I try in the next 12 months?

_____

_____

_____

_____

_____

What subjects do I want to learn more about or research?

_____

_____

_____

_____

_____

Chapter 4

The Conceptualization

Thought is the seed of action; but action is as much its second form as thought is its first.

Ralph Waldo Emerson, in "Art", in Society and Solitude (1870)

After you have become aware of an idea, you need to immediately condense it to the lower frequency level that will allow you to express it in words: thought. Transforming the gaseous idea into liquid, fluid, touchable thought requires two steps.

Capture Your Idea

Ideas are fast and they are fleeting. Like dreams, they will fade away very quickly if you do not immediately capture them. The simplest thing you need to do is to capture your idea immediately, not later, not "when I get home" not "next week" but immediately, in a notebook. For this purpose, you need to get into the habit of carrying around a notebook with you at all times. A note on your smartphone might do, but I would encourage you to use pen and paper as much as possible. You may not always be able to capture your idea with logical words. Sometimes, you will only be able to condense your idea in a drawing. You might need to doodle or jot down words that express feelings or sounds. You may want to staple an article from a newspaper or a print out something from the Internet, scrapbook style.

At this stage, it is very important to capture your idea in the first modality that comes easiest to you. A notebook will allow you to do that much easier than an electronic keyboard, although that might come useful as well when you don't have your notebook with you. You may also use a recorder. The important thing is to keep it exploratory and free. Don't worry about logic, order or style. Just record everything that comes to your mind

The habit of carrying around a notebook, while deceptively simple, may be the single most important thing you can do to start your journey into the materialization of ideas. Personally, it changed my life. I have always had a lot of creative ideas. But I never had a notebook with me. Taking notes has always been a burden for me, I have always preferred to keep things in my mind and I thought I was perfectly capable of doing so. But I had not yet understood the fleeting, gaseous dream like nature of ideas and for this reason, I probably lost a lot of my ideas on the way. Then, one day, someone gifted me with a small diary. I was sitting at a café waiting for someone. I didn't have a book with me and, tired of checking my blackberry, I took out the diary and wrote down a few items that were just crossing my mind. The next day, I looked at what I had written and on that basis of these words, I started preparing three new articles which then turned into a book.

Since then, I always carry a notebook. I urge you to do the same. You can use anything from a cheap supermarket notebook to an expensive leather covered journal.

Then, capture your ideas everywhere. Remember, ideas do not reveal themselves only in meetings. Ideas emerge when you are walking on the street, reading an article, taking a shower, driving, daydreaming, getting dressed or gazing out of the window during a taxi or bus drive. Make sure your notebook is near you.

Conceptualize your Idea

Conceptualizing your idea means unfolding your initial vision into a concept, expressing it in words, creating a world around it, linking it to your other ideas and projects. One of the techniques that help you go through this process is known as mind mapping. A *mind map* is a visual diagram used to represent concepts and ideas in a nonhierarchical form. You write down a keyword or picture representing the main issue or idea in the center of a blank page, and then associated ideas, words, or concepts into the map radially around this center node.

Mind mapping is one great way of conceptualizing, but there are also other methods. You may make a list, a diagram, a flow chart, a drawing, anything that your brain can conceive and that helps you express your idea in words and concepts and associate it with other ideas.

Consolidate your Ideas

The second step is going back to look at what you wrote and consolidating it. Open a word document or any other tool that works well for you and expand your idea into comprehensible words. This exercise is to allow you to grasp in comprehensible words the main outline of the idea, crystallizing it and building it into a more definite shape that can be "held" and worked with, but is still malleable, like a fluid.

Then search your inbox, post its, email box, post its, journal entries, for anything that you could connect to that idea. Consolidate everything in the same document.

If you work in a corporate environment, you will likely have a lot of digital content flowing through your inbox, and some resources or references connected to your idea might be scattered around in various emails. You should aggregate the content of all relevant emails into one document and save it together with the core document where you have put down your ideas. The most important thing is to aggregate everything in a place where you can easily find it, and create a structure around it. Take all your random notes and organize them into a concept. Keep feeding the concept by remembering to add any new thought to the structure you have created.

I find it very easy to work with word documents because I am a writer and most of my ideas can be expressed in words. However you might find that other consolidation methods work better for you. For instance, you may prefer using a tool like google wave. My husband, who is a very creative and visual entrepreneur, likes to touch things and see them in colors. He enjoys creating physical folders with colourful post it notes.

Insight: How I organize my ideas

I will give you a personal example of how I consolidate my ideas.

Whenever I have a new idea I give it a name and create a word document where I dump all my thoughts – taking them from my paper and pen notebook and expanding on them. I save that word document under a specific folder with the same name. It is very easy from there to keep expanding with more documents or concepts.

For example, when I first had the idea for this book I created a word file called "Ideas to reality" and saved it under a folder called "Ideas to reality". The first word document I created soon became a book proposal. From that, I created a second document which became the manuscript. I then created a subfolder called "research" and created a document where I dumped all research and resources I was planning to use. Then, I created another word document called "ideas to reality coaching project" where I consolidated my ideas about a coaching program dedicated to helping people make things happen.

My windows explorer now looks like this:

Documents
    Ideas in Reality
        Book
            Manuscript
            Book Proposal
            Graphic
             [Book Cover etc]
            Research
        Keynotes
            [Client A, client B etc]
            Coaching Project
            Coaching Program outline
        Articles
            Work in progress
            Published

Setting Goals

When I work with people to help them make their ideas happen, I am often asked whether the materialization phase requires setting a specific goal and how you set that goal. Yes! You need to have a clear vision in your mind of what you want to realize. At this stage, it is time to develop your idea into a concept, setting a defined goal that you can write, express and share with others in logical terms. This is when your goal becomes refined and tangible. How do you set your goal? First of all, your idea will have manifested itself in some kind of vision, picture. For example, you might have been listening to a piece of music you love and suddenly an idea flashed through your mind: how beautiful would it be to play this piece, and pictured yourself playing it on the piano. That was your idea. This is the start of your goal setting: you decide you want to learn to play the piano, and your goal is to learn to play that particular piece of music.

Second, in the conceptualization phase, ask yourself WHY you want to transform this particular idea in reality. What is your purpose for wanting to play the piano? Do you want to become a composer? Play in concerts? Entertain your family? What is your purpose for the new business you want to set up? For the book you want to write? The new product you want to create? When you know "your why," it becomes incredibly easy to set a specific goal of what you want to achieve.

THE ROADMAP TO

CONCEPTUALIZE YOUR IDEAS

Capture

Keep a journal, notebook or electronic diary to record regularly your flashes, ideas, insights and thoughts

Capture, capture, capture, all the time, everywhere

Where will I capture my ideas?

_____

_____

_____

_____

_____

Conceptualize

As you go about your day, think of which other ideas or projects you have thought of are associated with your new idea. Whether you have generated your idea in a meeting brainstorming session or a chance conversation or in an article or eureka moment in the shower, link it to a specific project.

Mind map, create a structure and a project. Then reduce your map to a proper form. Pare your map down to express your most cogent insights and reorder the branches to reflect a new organization of your thoughts.

Can my idea be transformed into a project? Or, what bigger (new or existing) projects can my idea be linked to?

_____

_____

_____

_____

_____

Consolidate

Take all the ideas around you – sentences in emails, sketches in notebooks, scribbles on post it notes and consolidate them.

Create a file for each individual idea.

Create a file even if the idea is not yet actionable. I have a folder in my computer called "work in progress".

Re-read your ideas or recorded thoughts. You should refer to these records from time to time and you'll probably be amazed at how many interesting things you will find. When I first decided it was time to start writing again, I went back to my files on my computer. I was astonished at how much I had already done in terms of research, notes, writing. There hadn't been one week where I hadn't written something.

Create a system that is easy for use to access and don't hesitate to change it when things get more complicated

Where will I consolidate and structure my idea? (computer, paper archive). How does my system need to be reorganized?

_____

_____

_____

_____

_____

Setting Goals

What triggered this idea?

_____

_____

_____

_____

_____

What was my initial vision?

_____

_____

_____

_____

_____

Why do I want to make this idea happen?

_____

_____

_____

_____

_____

Chapter 5

The Materialization

I don't believe the muse visits you. I believe you visit the muse.
Michael Lewis

I get impatient when I see friends and colleagues come up with great ideas, only to become distracted by the demands of their life and then conclude they have no time to pursue their dreams. Although most people think their problem is a lack of creativity, they are actually failing to follow up on a creative idea. Pursuing and actually realizing an idea is very rare.

There are several reasons for this. One reason is that putting an idea into practice can seem like a huge amount of work. Even if it's a small idea, most of us see nothing but potential obstacles when we imagine taking action.

Another reason can be fear of moving out of our current, comfortable space. A third reason is that the adventurous, creative mind often likes to pride itself on its creativity quotient, often seeing the actual realization of an idea as meaningless. Creative people view themselves, and society views them, as a unique bunch. And finally, as discussed in Chapter 1, often the execution of ideas is suffocated by the lack of external support from an environment that, consciously or subconsciously, perceives pursuing a new idea as a threat or as a waste of time.

Switching Gears

In the third phase of realization, you are dealing with a project. In order to be turned into reality, every idea must be associated with a project, whether personal (planning a vacation) or professional (a new project launch).

Curiosity and mental wanderlust is what fuels ideas, but making them happen requires commitment, project management and execution.

What you need to keep in mind, and accept, for it is a difficult realization to accept, is that the source of your ideas, your creativity, is a completely different mental state, force and reality level from what makes you productive and able to execute those ideas.

In this phase of idea materialization, your idea needs to be molded and transformed into something real. It needs to be condensed to solid. If you have an artistic mind, you might feel that in the process your idea loses some of its original beauty, it's not as pure and lovely as when you conceived it, in its formless airiness. However, the stepping down of an idea into the physical world is what allows you to share that idea with the world. Ideas are useless unless they make an impact or, they affect someone's life. It is a fact that someone with an average idea but amazing organizational skills will make a greater impact than someone who has a groundbreaking idea but is disorganized and unable to materialize that idea, condense it, solidify it and make it happen.

In order to make your idea happen, you therefore need to switch from right brain thinking to left brain thinking. All of us have both. All of us can tap into the power of both. Going back to my consolidation metaphor, you simply need to work on a different frequency level. You are now working to bring your fluid to a solid state level, you need to compress matter and slow down energy levels. Another way to describe this process is to imagine that you're racing on your mountain bike and you will need to switch gears depending on the type and inclination of the road you are negotiating.

The Key Elements of Materialization

Self Leadership

Once you have generated a new idea, you need to stay productive, accountable and in control. For any idea to become reality, it must be treated as an enterprise. Whether you work in a corporation or on your own, whether you are writing a book, producing a work of art, implementing a new invention or applying a new business idea, you are an entrepreneur who needs to make ideas happen.

You will therefore need substantive time and mental loyalty to avoid being sidetracked by the constant flow of urgent matters that arise every day and capture your attention.

Self-leadership is the most important quality you need in this phase of creation in order to turn your idea into reality. We often see leadership as the ability to lead others; however, leading oneself is what comes first, and the ability to lead oneself derives mainly from self awareness. Self awareness - a thorough understanding of your values, mental patterns, strengths and weaknesses - will allow you to understand and deal with your inner conflicts, which are the biggest obstacles in reaching your goals.

Inner conflicts are the result of competing claims on your energy and attention. By knowing yourself, you learn to work with your limitations and strengths in order to make a conscious choice between those competing claims.

Becoming a master in managing your time is an essential skill of self leadership. Learning how to master your energy, knowing which activities feed you energy and which sap your energy, is just as important. Managing your time and energy ensures that you do not fall into a state of impulsive work flow, where you only try to stay afloat and therefore aren't very productive.

Support from others

Mustering the stamina to pursue bold and long term ideas also requires a solid dose of self reliance and the mental independence to set up your own personal system of rewards. Making ideas happen requires patience, stamina, dedication. Success will only come later and during the materialization phase you will likely have a period of time where you will not see any results. If you rely on outside assurances and rewards (what "success" is in the eyes of others) you will very likely feel like giving up your project. Therefore, one of the most important aspects of materializing your idea is your ability to unplug from the traditional rewards system and embrace your own set of values, going for some time without "success" in the eyes of others.

I have seen this happen many times when friends as well as my own husband decided to leave a well paid and comfortable corporate career to set up their own company. Any entrepreneurial venture is an uphill road. The first few years are likely not to generate profits. If you are pursuing a big idea, such as a new entrepreneurial venture, you may need to downscale your expenses, your social commitments and your lifestyle and give up, or suspend, a traditional career path. Other people will often ask you whether it is worth the sacrifice and may let you know that they think what you are doing does not make sense.

Hitting up against the wall of social expectations is not easy. If you are not aware of this and have made a conscious choice to deal with it, your vision and idea might crumble when faced with a war against the short term reward system that permeates our lives. It is hard to say no to constant demands from our daily life, jobs, social circle and families for a bigger, longer term goal that we cannot see. If you believe in your idea, it is critical that you make a conscious choice to set up your own system of rewards.

Depending on how innovative your idea is, whether it's a new business process, or a new venture you want to take in your life, you will face a fair amount of pressure from your close group - colleagues, business partners, family. Whenever you change something in your normal routine or schedule, you can rest assured that people around you will see it with suspicion and challenge it. In order to overcome this, challenge yourself to calmly withstand the social pressures, and the self doubts that will inevitably come from the people around you. Slowly, you will win over the most aggressive opposition. Remember: people always criticize at first, but ultimately greatly admire someone who has a strong mind.

However, you must keep in mind that there are some people you will need to win over if you want to progress with your project. Without these people, you might be trailing down a too difficult road. For example, you'll need the support of your spouse in the case of a personal project, or the major stakeholders in your company if you are working on a new idea in a corporate context.

At the beginning of this new project, make a realistic list of which assurances and support you need and from whom, and think of a strategy to win them over.

Once you have made the list of people whose assurances you need, it is easy to put everyone else on the list of the assurances you do not need. This will also help you disregard any irrelevant criticism or resistance!

Getting organized

Organization is about applying order to the many elements of a creative project.

The most important organizational element is structure. Whenever we generate a new, exciting, beautiful idea, it is natural to shun structure as a way of protecting the free flowing, dreamy, nature of the idea. However when you get to this third stage - the manifestation stage - structure is essential.

In order to start enjoying organization, I suggest you use an organization method that you enjoy and do not force yourself to use something you really hate. For example, I am not a fan of Excel and prefer Word tables, although I am aware that Excel makes some functions easier. However, in those few occasions when I let myself be convinced to use excel to keep track of my to do list, I hated it so much I stopped keeping track. When I switched to a word table, I kept it constantly updated, even though the formatting required more work and I had limited inputting options. The aesthetic of your tools may also matter. If you are a visual person, when you have a project that is tracked on a beautiful chart or elegant sketchbook, you are more likely to follow through.

One simple system that I use daily that has helped me immensely with all my projects is to keep a notebook, diary or even just scrap paper on your desk and every day sketch your to do list on the top of the page. As the day goes by and I get things done, I cross out the activities I have completed. If I haven't finished something, I carry it over to the next day and write it down again. Especially when working on a large project that involves several activities, writing them down helps narrow your focus and avoid a sense of being overwhelmed. It also frees your mind: you no longer need to think about what you need to do, you have it written down for easy reference, you can just concentrate on doing things.

If you are working on a project that involves other people, it is essential to create an owner for the action steps, whether yourself or another person, and hold them accountable.

In order to get things done, you also need to create windows of uninterrupted time where you simply go through your to do list and one by one tackle the actions you have written down. I have addressed the issue of distraction and information overload extensively in my book *The Principle of Relevance.* What I would like to convey to you here is that you need to make a conscious decision, set an intention, to extract yourself from a linear, reactionary work flow where you spend your time responding to inputs as they come in (emails, messages, phone calls, interruptions of any sort) in a misguided attempt at being efficient. Have you ever noticed how your level of interruption increases in direct proportion to your level of availability? The more you respond to emails, for example, the more emails you get back. This isn't necessarily because people want to communicate more with you; it is more likely because the communication going on in those emails is not structured enough to be sufficient to address the issue without a stream of consciousness back and forth.

In order to avoid being interrupted all the time, make an effort to be structured and complete in your communications. This in turn forces people to do the same with you!

Attention spans also seem to relentlessly shrink in the digital age. The meditation exercises I suggest in the idea generation phase will have a great impact in increasing your attention span and deepen the ability to intelligently focus exclusively on a task or action rather than mindlessly multitasking. We all have to acknowledge a relentless shortening of the period of time we can spend on a particular project or situation.

Side by side with striving to improve your focus capabilities, you must become conscious of your attention span-- how long it is how it works, and learn to use it to your advantage. For example, if you know that your maximum focus attention span is 15 minutes, why not divide the task you need to perform into smaller bits that fit into that 15 minute block and schedule minor activities in between (phone calls you need to return; a simple search you want to carry out on the Internet, etc).

I find that writing down a plan (or list of activities) for those flickering moments when attention to the main task fades is an incredibly useful way to make the most of my attention waves. It also helps me focus back on the primary task. Once the list of minor activities such as a minor "urgent" task to do, an email to be answered, a phone call returned, the daily news checked, you have nothing left but to go back and refocus.

For this purpose, I usually keep two lists in my daily organization: the "urgent and minor things" list and the "important and major things" list. I do both. While I live by the *7 Habits of Highly Successful People* principle of differentiating urgent from important (if you only hoard urgent items you will never get the other things done, because urgent tasks create more urgent tasks) in the digital age it is sometimes difficult to avoid the urgent and immediate. So keep two lists! You will see major improvements in how many things you get done during the day.

A heightened awareness of my attention span and how to use it has become incredibly beneficial since having my son. As all parents must know, with a baby, the slots I had during the day to work and write were very few. If I wanted to make the most of them, I needed to become a master at being extremely focused and making the most of my attention span. By following the aforementioned principles, I was able to keep writing even during the first months of my baby's life. I kept a running list of things to do, divided between the major (writing my book, submitting an article, preparing a speech) and minor (for example responding to an email, checking comments on my facebook fan page) and effectively placed each task in a time slot according to my attention span and focused around when my baby was sleeping. When I felt I was focused, I would write or prepare a speech. When I was unfocused and distracted, I would carry out minor task and tick them off the list. This kept my work going at a pace which surprised everyone, even I!

Rituals

While idea generation thrives on unstructured, open spaces, and a non- routine, implementing your project in the materialization phase may required you to work in a completely different location or situation. Creating a ritual for your materialization phase work can be very effective in helping you settle into the state of mind you want for this type of work. Working in a particular workspace, office, time of the day or as a follow up to some other activity (for example, after reading the morning news) can create a ritual that helps you flow through your tasks.

For example, while idea generation happens to me everywhere, although mostly after a quiet meditation session, while jogging or walking outside or while riding my motorcycle and I conceptualize my ideas mostly while sitting on the couch and sharing them with my husband, I have a daily ritual for my materialization phase.

I usually do materialization work (writing a book or articles, preparing a speech or training, structuring a project) in the morning, after breakfast. I read and answer emails from clients and journalists for half hour to shift me in the right mental working zone for materialization work. I use a lavender scent in the room and sometimes, though not always, I listen to classical music.

Project plateaus

A project plateau is a moment during your materialization phase when you feel that you just cannot go on any longer. You may become thoroughly bored with your idea - and the effort required to execute it. Typically, you fall out of love with your idea, which does not seem so innovative or so bright anymore. Or you may run out of resources (money, time, energy) or resourcefulness (your ability to find resources even when there seem to be none immediately available) and feel you no longer wish to make the effort. You may resent the time and commitment that your project requires. Whatever the underlying feeling, project plateaus happen inevitably. At the beginning of the realization of a new idea, there is always a moment of great energy where things seem to progress swiftly. It is like a honeymoon period, when you are in love with your idea and are ready to take any step to materialize it.

Then as you move further along, there comes a time when you lose the sparkly feeling and wonder whether you really want to continue spending the time and energy. This happens because you may be overwhelmed with the sheer quantity of things to do, have a conflict with other commitments, because you see no major progress for some time, or because you are just plain bored with your idea or all of the above. No matter what your feeling is, this is the most critical point in your idea materialization phase. If you give up at this stage, you will never make your idea happen. It is like most romantic relationships: when the honeymoon phase fades, there is a moment of crisis where you question whether it makes sense to continue the relationship or move on to another one. Only if you get past this moment can you can develop a true, deep, intimate relationship.

There is one important lesson I learned while I was writing my first book and reached the inevitable project plateau. Your thoughts will not change your emotions but actions will. If you just get into motion without giving yourself the time to think or question, you will move on with your action plan. This the time when having a clearly identified action plan will be the most beneficial to you. To traverse the plateau phase without being swallowed by it, you must keep in constant motion.

If you are able to traverse a project plateau, your idea materialization phase will thrive. Also, the manifestation of ideas rarely happens in a linear structured way. It often happens in spurts: this means you may go back and forth and have several project plateaus. However, the first plateau is the most difficult to ride. Once you have successfully gone through the first plateau and deepened the relationship and commitment to your idea, any other plateau will be much easier to overcome.

Here are some ideas to ensure you keep moving through your idea materialization phase during a plateau:

Cross-examine yourself

If you are stuck, ask yourself why this has happened. Are you missing some important resources that you need to find in order to move forward? Are you scared of taking action? Are you lazy? Are you waiting for perfection? Are you worried about the costs or risks of taking action? Is there something in your mood or emotions that is holding you back? Be ruthlessly honest with yourself. Write down the reasons for your procrastination. Most of them will be excuses but some of them will require you to find the right resources to overcome the problem.

Take a Thinking Pause

For a few days, give your brain some space to process what it has done so far and generate new ideas on how to move forward. Then go through the process of putting them in action.

Phone a Friend

Reach a friend, mentor or even a professional coach, someone who can be a sounding board for you. Discuss the issues with them and openly share the problem that you have in moving forward. Choose someone who is discreet, honest and forthright, who will challenge your views, provide you with perspective and ask questions that move you forward.

Remind yourself of your final goal

Write down your final goal and frame it somewhere visible. Also, you can share your project with someone you admire. Telling someone you admire that you will do something will give you a sense of commitment.

Go back to your initial inspiration

What inspired you in the first place? Where did you get your first idea? Go back to that place, listen to that same piece of music, reread that book or article, have a conversation with that particular person, bring yourself back to that moment of magic which sparked your idea initially.

Do something – get into motion

There are times when it is very difficult if not impossible to make the right decision. Under these circumstances you have two major options. You can keep analyzing, thinking, talking, looking for more information and waiting to see if things become clearer. Or you can deliberately take some action, see what happens and then revisit the decision.   As I wrote earlier, thoughts don't change your emotions but actions do. Write down two or three things you need to do next and get in motion!

Break It Down

Break down your project into smaller steps, pick one, and do it.

Fuel Your Idea with New Ideas

As we will see in Chapter 6, this is a process in motion. While you are working on the materialization phase of your idea, you will fuel it with more ideas and go back and forth through the consolidation process. So when you are stuck, take an idea generation break and relive the poetry of generating new ideas that will fuel your project and reignite your passion.

Other people

In every project, you will need to involve other people. This may be necessary because you need support with technical skills (You may need to hire an attorney, a secretary, a PR agent, architect, or a shipping company. You may also want to involve other people to harness the driving force of a community, or partnership. The moment you engage someone else in your project, whether it is a partner or hired help you become accountable to them and they to you.

One of the most powerful things I did when I had the idea of creating my most successful project - the Women Leadership Project (www.womenleadershipproject.com) was to share my idea with another professional woman whom I trusted would be able to add value and perspective to the project. Her experience, cheering and support helped me keep my vision and make that idea in reality. Therefore, involving others, on top of helping you fill the gap on technical skills you lack, may help you ride project plateaus.

Pick carefully the people you share your idea with to ensure that they are reliable partners who understand the three phases of the process of transforming ideas into reality.

Insight: Think about Intellectual Property Protection

Not all ideas can be protected as intellectual property. Most of the ideas you will generate might be applications of existing processes to a particular situation you are dealing with. However, if your idea is original and innovative, you should certainly strive to protect it. In order to do so, you have to obtain sound information as to whether your idea can be protected and how. Is your idea a patentable invention? Is it copyrighted? Is it a trade secret? Is it a business process? Generally speaking, works of art, books, music are copyrightable materials. In order to apply for a patent, you need an invention. A business idea might be more difficult to protect with a registration. However, make sure you evaluate carefully whomever you share your idea with, and if necessary, ask them to sign a non disclosure agreement (a short contract that binds them to keep the information you use with them confidential and not use it in any other way except as agreed with you).

Promoting Your Idea

Marketing your idea and building a promotion platform around it is the last step in your materialization phase. This phase, while it can actually be a lot of fun once you get the hang of it, is not easy for most people. In my case, for example, as an attorney, I had to overcome my preconceived notion that marketing is bad and unethical (probably due to the fact that overt marketing is forbidden to lawyers in most countries). The reality is that for every idea you materialize, you need buyers and stakeholders, even if that only means getting your spouse on board with your new project of becoming a kung fu black belt, which will require you to train twice a week after work. Also, if you need other people to be involved in your project, you need to get others to understand and support the idea as though it were their own. If you are lacking the marketing skills you need, learning how to properly market your idea can be an idea within the idea which can help increase your creative fire!

THE ROADMAP TO

MATERIALIZE YOUR IDEAS

Self Leadership

Which activities and situations fuel my energy and which sap it?

_____

_____

_____

_____

_____

Support from Others

Which assurances and support do I need and from whom? How am I going to win them over? Which assurances do I not need?

_____

_____

_____

_____

_____

Organization

Use an organization method that you enjoy.

Use a notebook and sketch your schedule for every day on the top of the page

Create windows of time dedicated to uninterrupted focus. Notice that your level of interruption increases in direct proportion to your level of availability.

Use your attention span to your advantage.

Break down your tasks and avoid multitasking.

Regularly, assess how you spend your time and eliminate irrelevant activities.

Questions for You

Which organization method do I enjoy? Which will I use?

_____

_____

_____

_____

_____

How long is my attention span? How can I use it to my advantage by scheduling minor tasks during my attention span breaks?

_____
_____
_____
_____
_____

How will I create stretches of time of uninterrupted focus?

_____
_____
_____
_____
_____

Which irrelevant activities can I eliminate?

_____
_____
_____
_____
_____

Rituals

What anchors facilitate my transition to idea materialization phase?

_____

_____

_____

_____

_____

What rituals will I create to help my flow of work?

_____

_____

_____

_____

_____

Project Plateaus

Who will I call in a project plateau? What readings/thoughts/environments will I go back to?

_____

_____

_____

_____

_____

Other People

Who will I work with and what will I delegate? How will I hold them accountable?

_____

_____

_____

_____

_____

Marketing

Who will I market my project to?

_____

_____

_____

_____

_____

How will I market my project?

_____

_____

_____

_____

_____

Chapter 6

Putting Everything Into Motion

Making an idea happen is an ongoing process that will often require you to shift frequencies from idea generation to materialization. New ideas will fuel your project as you move along and your project will in turn fuel the generation of new ideas. Even during an intense phase of realization of a project you might have new ideas, whether related to the project itself, for example ideas on how to market it, ideas on how to improve it or sometimes unrelated. You will have to be flexible and constantly move from one phase to the other.

Every time this happens, go back and repeat the steps of consolidation. Conceptualize your idea into thought, and then incorporate that concept into your action plan.

This process is invaluable as often in the process of realizing an idea, you might not have the entire plan figured out and you might need to make decisions based on some unknown. Often ideas that show up in the middle of the plan can provide solutions that will bring your project forward with a leap.

In a phase of realization of an idea, the constant process of going back and forth from idea to thought to project, from gas to liquid to solid and back can open your mind to a level of flexibility that you might not have experienced before.

So whether your dream is to create a new business, implement and entrepreneurial idea, follow a creative pursuit (like writing a book) or develop a life enhancing habit (like exercising), you might need to stretch beyond your comfort zone. You will need to develop creativity if you are mainly practical, master the art of execution and organization if you are mainly creative, and continue to work on developing your self awareness.

This may also mean, literally, using different physical locations for the various phases. It is true that idea generation thrives in different situations and locations from consolidation and manifestation: ideas appear more easily in open spaces while you are relaxed, while project management and tasks are more effectively carried out in structured spaces. I invite you to explore and find what specific conditions are best for you. Find what level of brightness, noise and ambiance, which kind of music, which objects, what time of the day fit with a specific phase and use them as anchors. Sit on your terrace to find ideas, go back to your office to implement them. Listen to Tibetan music in the morning or evening to access your muse, turn up the techno in the middle of the day to go through your task list.

Your idea is on its way to becoming reality!

Visit

www.stefanialucchetti.com

Sign up

to Stefania Lucchetti's blog and participate to the discussion.